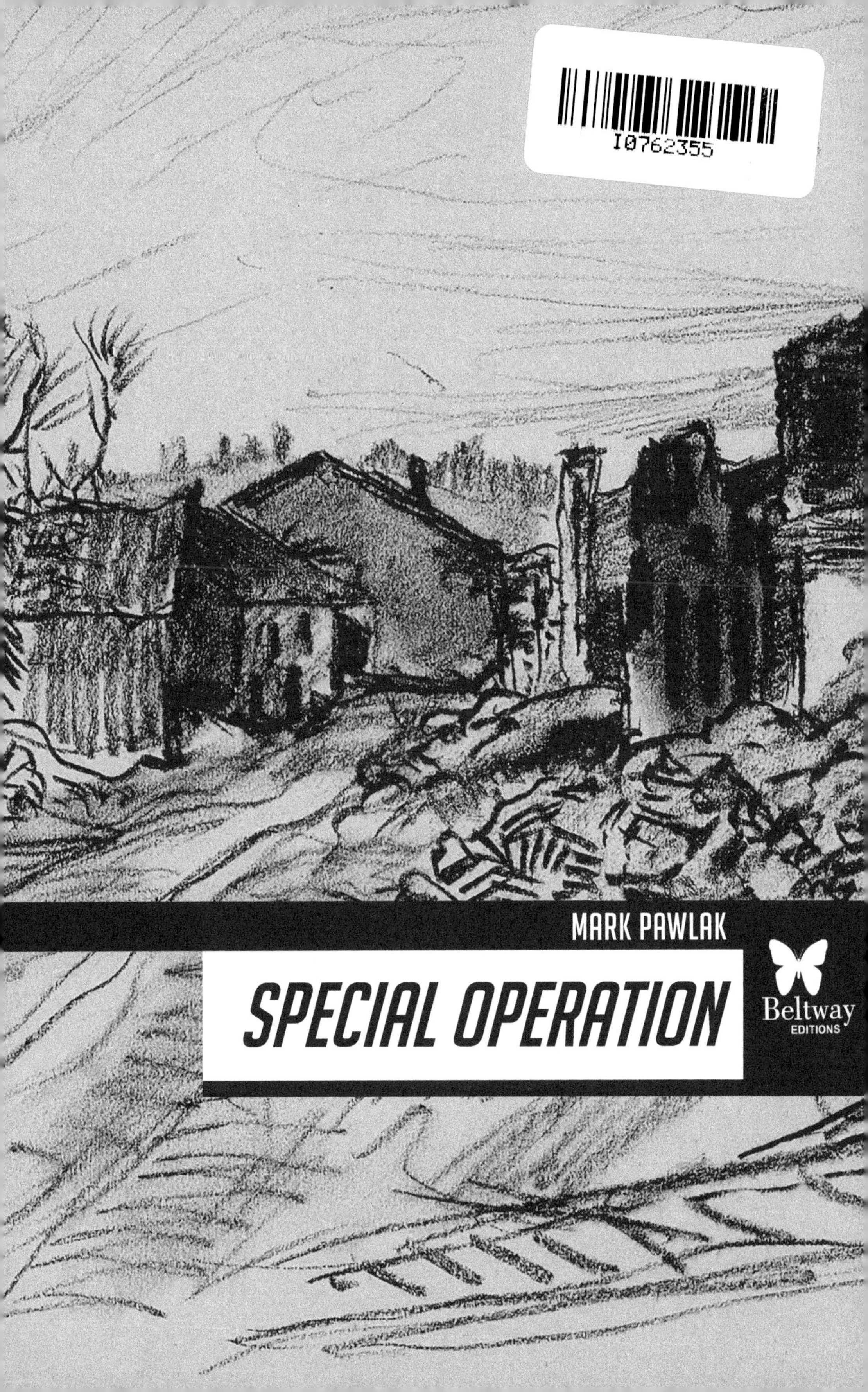

MARK PAWLAK

SPECIAL OPERATION

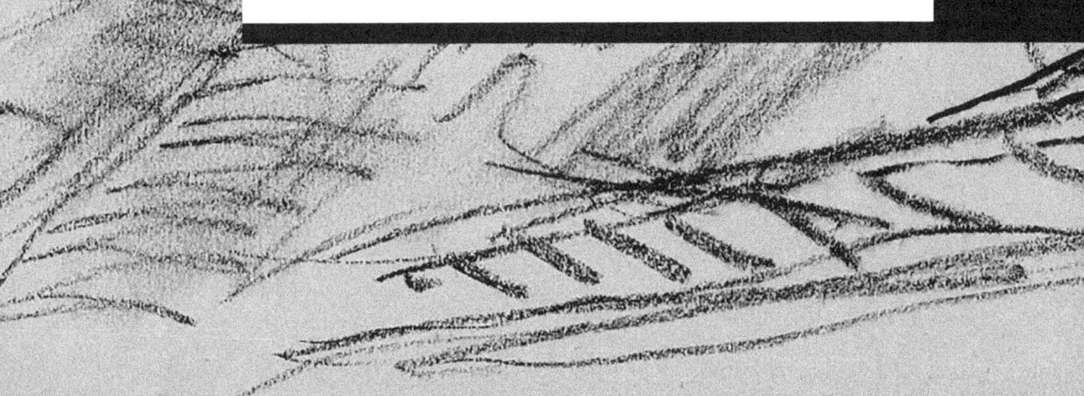

MARK PAWLAK

SPECIAL OPERATION

Beltway
EDITIONS

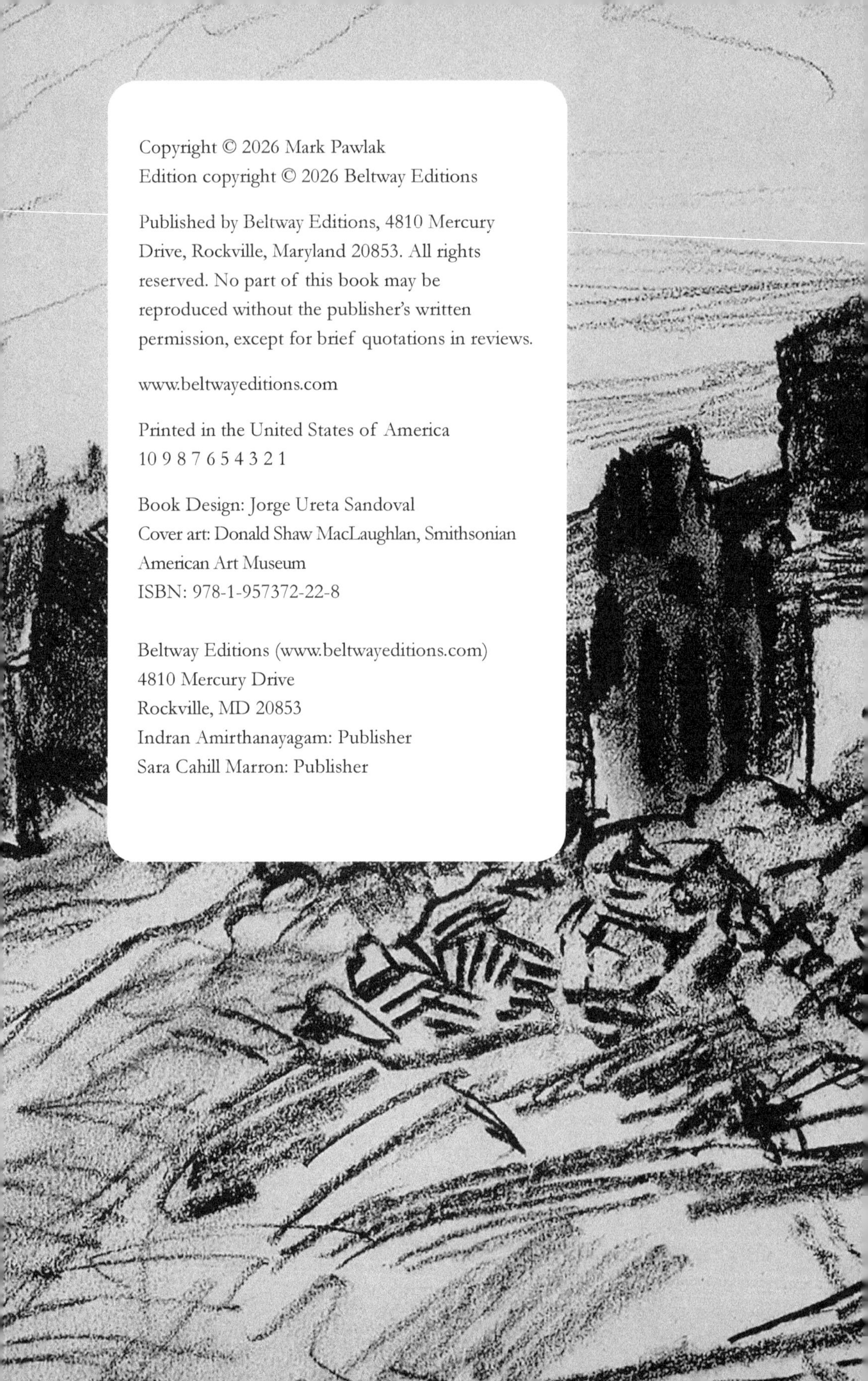

www.beltwayeditions.com

Printed in the United States of America
10 9 8 7 6 5 4 3 2 1

Book Design: Jorge Ureta Sandoval
Cover art: Donald Shaw MacLaughlan, Smithsonian American Art Museum
ISBN: 978-1-957372-22-8

Beltway Editions (www.beltwayeditions.com)
4810 Mercury Drive
Rockville, MD 20853
Indran Amirthanayagam: Publisher
Sara Cahill Marron: Publisher

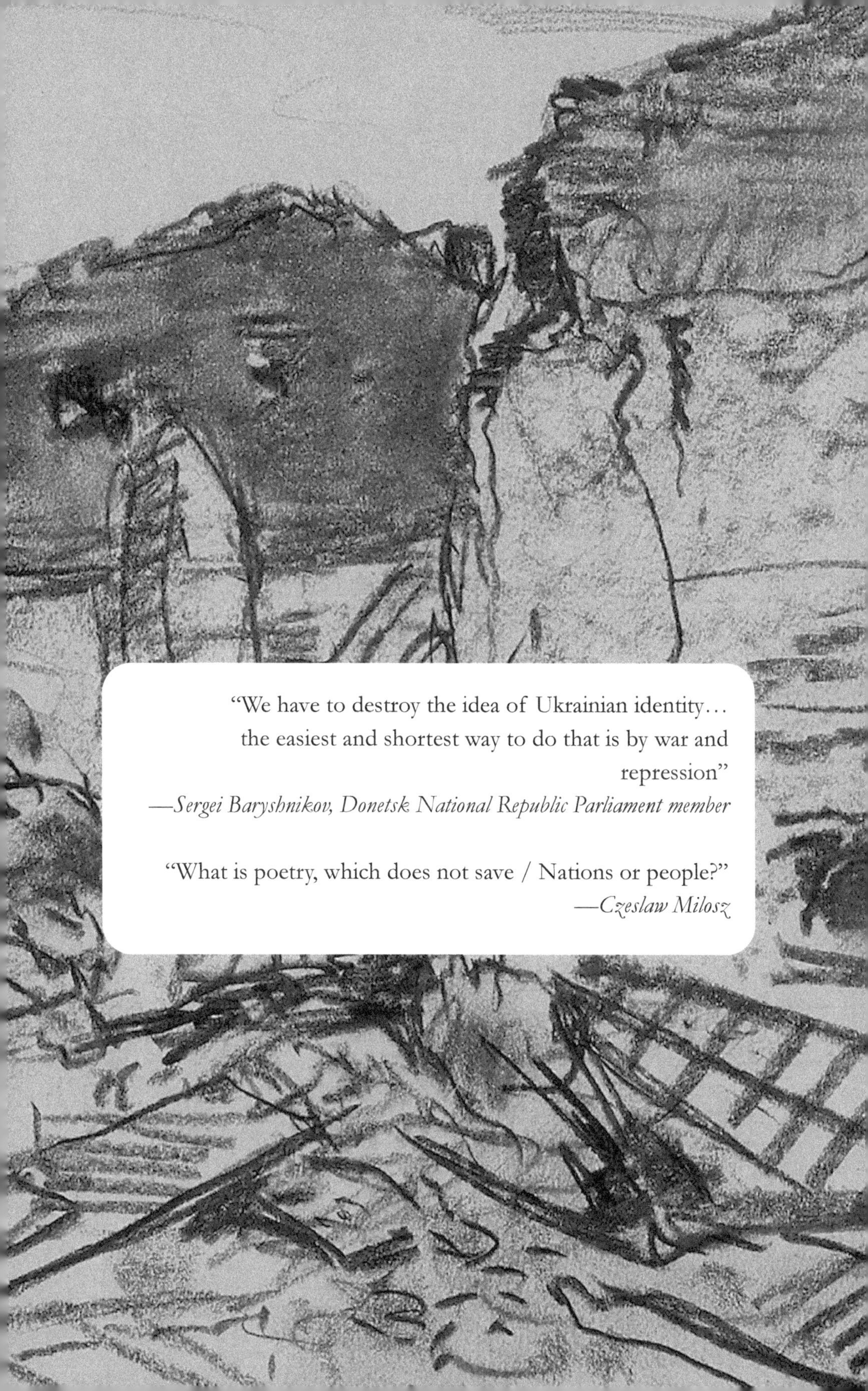

"We have to destroy the idea of Ukrainian identity… the easiest and shortest way to do that is by war and repression"
—*Sergei Baryshnikov, Donetsk National Republic Parliament member*

"What is poetry, which does not save / Nations or people?"
—*Czeslaw Milosz*

TABLE OF CONTENTS

MARK PAWLAK

SPECIAL OPERATION

Prologue: Don't Worry

As Russia's first battalions attack Kharkiv,
her older sister calls from her home in Moscow.
"Don't worry, Putin says this is his 'Special Operation'
—it's only military targets."

"Good," she says. "So please ask him
why his Operation's missile struck
your niece's kindergarten."

I

Primer

Babusya, beware!
It is no bumblebee
hovering above your house.
This sting is lethal.

*

On the horizon, a flock
approaches swiftly from the east:
Sound the alarm!
Take shelter!

*

Wailing sirens, screaming:
missile! incoming!
Pray the warnings
never come too late.

*

Darkness descends:
you survived another day, Babusya!
Darkness descends:
a new opportunity to die in your sleep!

Collateral Damage

> "Others can now identify the type and caliber
> of weapon from its mere sound. But...
> we were just beginning to discover the meaning of war."
> —Victoria Amelina, *Homo Oblivious*

On the way home with a few provisions,
still clutching his plastic bag,
face down on the sidewalk
in a pool of blood.

Special Delivery: From Russia with Love

Cost: $3 million.
Weight: 4.5 tons.
Range: 500 kilometers.
Speed: 2000 kilometers per second.
Accuracy: 5 meter radius.
Payload: cluster bomb, fuel-air explosive, or bunker-buster.
Inscription (hand painted): "For the children."

"The strike on Kramatorsk was a real beauty."
—Colonel General Andry Karapolov on Russian TV:
"I bow my head to those who planned it.
Not a blow but a song.
My old military heart rejoices."

Casualties: 63 killed (including 9 children),
150 injured (including 35 children).

Erasure

"On February 24th. The word 'Never' was erased."

—Volodymyr Zalesnkyy

After the last war,
the words "Never Again!"
were on the lips of survivors;

were painted in black letters
on the brick facades of new construction
rising from the rubble: "Never Again."

But when artillery shells and missiles
demolish buildings,
they create by erasure—

as this new war demonstrates—a new slogan
on brick facades and survivors' lips:
"Again!"

Old Suitcases

Those old suitcases in your closet, Babusya,
those two tattered suitcases,
one with a broken strap,

those suitcases your mother
placed in back of the closet
after the last war …

it's time to drag them out again, Babusya;
time to dust them off,
repair the strap.

II

"Never think that war, no matter how necessary or how justified, is not a crime. Ask the infantry and ask the dead."

—Ernest Hemingway, *For Whom the Bell Tolls*

Advance

> "Death, no doubt, dug/ and watered these deep furrows / where men are planted."
>
> —Julien Vocance, *One Hundred Visions of War*

No-Man's-Land a century ago:
barren swath hundreds of yards wide
between lines of barbed wire and trenches:
muddy, cratered, littered
with men's corpses, horse carcasses.

No-Man's-Land today:
a mile-wide swath between trenches:
muddy, cratered, seeded with land mines,
littered with men's corpses and
charred remains of armored vehicles.

Somme 1916; Donbas 2022:
Western civilization's great advance!

Reaper

> "...worm-ridden earth will fill my mouth and eyes
> and roots will pierce through my body."
>
> —Miklos Radnoti, "*War Diary*" (Tr. Gina Gönczi)

1.

Row upon row
Shoulder high sunflowers

Row upon row
bowed heads heavy

Row upon row
with unharvested seeds:

Who worked these fields?
A different reaper.

2.

Wooden crosses
on mounds of earth

in neatly spaced rows
far as the eye can see:

regimented in death
where in life chaos reigned.

Fresh Recruits

They exchange:
prison uniforms for flak jackets,
shovels for assault rifles,
pick axes for bayonets
walled courtyard for crater-pocked fields.

They're paroled from barred cells to trenches:
starry sky overhead
and predator drones with night vision.

*

"They come in waves"/ storming trenches.
"They come in waves,"/ overwhelming defenders.
"They come in waves."
          / charging across fields littered with corpses
headlong into *the meat grinder.*

*

When their assault succeeds
and they occupy the enemy's trenches,
next to the dead they find cups of tea
still warm.

Duty

"The Bodies are all buried now/ Or rotted where they lay."

—Keith Wilson, *Graves Registry*

He ventures into battlefields
(moonless nights, rainy days, fog shrouds)
he ventures into battlefields
to retrieve bodies
"We must remember," he says,
"that even the dead have rights."

enemy soldiers
covered with frost
enemy soldiers
in bomb cratered,
enemy soldiers
sprawled on blasted tanks,
stinking corpses stacked up in trenches,
those in winter uniform top of the pile
those in summer camo underneath
"It's important for me to bring them all home"—
even his enemies.

No Christmas truce this war,
no hugs exchanged in fellowship,
no brandy traded for schnapps. Here
the transactions are in corpses, their countrymen for his—
solace for grieving mothers? Solace for weeping wives?
"We are humans," he says,
"and we must remember to remain human."

Bloodland

Gravediggers excavate yawning pits
to inter the bodies left behind
by the retreating enemy.

They take care
not to disturb the bones
of those massacred in previous wars.

Domicile

Table and chairs; sofa, ottoman, mattress;
wardrobe, bureau, family photos;
garish wallpaper, ceiling, four walls...

Table smashed/ chairs: snapped matchsticks/
sofa, ottoman, mattress smoldering/
wardrobe disemboweled/ bureau toppled/
wallpaper shrapnel-pocked/ ceiling gaping/
fourth wall sheared away...
Stage set for tragedy awaiting playwright:
title: *Domicile.*

Enter: woman in babushka with broom.
Sweeps wood (splinters), crockery (fragments),
glass (shards), masonry (chips) into neat piles;
bends to see smiling faces: (charred photos).

Photograph

Z—Russian military symbol for victory.

Not a single house or barn was left standing
after the Russians retreated:
branches snapped, trees stripped of leaves...

Surviving villagers who come out of hiding encounter
the results of the carnage: corpses
amid the rubble of flattened buildings and charred cars,

not only their neighbors and defenders,
but enemy soldiers, too,
the ones their comrades—fleeing in haste—left behind.

These, the villagers gathered up for a photograph
first arranging them in the shape of a Z.

The Gift

Don't be surprised, Babusya,
to find the homestead you had to flee
illuminated now:
moonlight through holes in the roof.

Come summer, the shattered door, burst windows,
shell pocked walls
will provide ventilation.

And your garden plot, Babusya,
won't need digging: already cratered, trenched,
it's well prepared for spring planting.

And, Babusya, don't be surprised by the gift
the retreating Russians left at your front gate:
that charred T4 tank signed with a Z.

Christmas in Kharkiv

Children search the heavens
for marauding drones, streaking missiles.

Families without Christmas cheer
huddle in basements, in shelters,

sing hymns, pray:
"Peace on earth, goodwill to men."

Tables set, feasts laid out
in basements, in shelters,

camo jackets draped over
the backs of empty chairs

set for those at the front, for the fallen.
There are no holidays in the trenches.

Kharkiv rings in the New Year with
sirens and explosions.

Survivor

"Like radiation, evil has a long half-life."
—Timothy Garton Ash

Now 98, she has survived Stalin's famine.
She knows what it's like to go without food.
Now, she tends her garden plot:
potatoes, cabbages, onions.

Rifle fire, explosions, occupation.
One Russian soldier shoots the family's barking dog.
"What have you done? That was our protector!"
"I'm your protector now," he says.

Rifle fire, explosions.
Separated from family, fleeing west alone,
no food, no water, on foot,
in house slippers.

Exploding artillery shells, cratered roads ...
she steps over dead bodies,
walks past cars, trucks:
blasted, smoldering.

Cars, trucks: blasted, smoldering,
roads littered with corpses
98, fleeing west in slippers...
She crosses herself; she prays.

98, in house slippers, no food, no water…,
she has no use, she says, for Russian "protectors."
Stalin's famine, Putin's invasion:
she's a survivor.

The Gardener

After the invaders were pushed back,
residents returned: a trickle.

Some buildings: repaired, reinhabited;
the bombed apartment tower torn down.
Shops reopened. On the streets
car, bus, bicycle traffic: as before.

Then the bombings began again;
the neighborhood emptied, again.
Except her: she never abandoned
her shell-pocked home.

Her son is at the front.
Now the only resident of her block,
she tends her garden,
the one she's kept for 30 years:

her hands weeding,
spade and pitchfork turning earth—
in the bomb craters
she plants new flowers.

All around: destruction;
in her apartment, order:
Czech crystal displayed
on top of her dresser.

"I have organized everything,"
she says, "according to my plans;"
"only the war is out of my control."

Fortitude

Kharkiv: beauty salon
where a young woman
with prosthetic fingers
is getting
some red nail polish.

Epilogue: "Bombweed"

> "Blitzed areas of London brimmed with pink swaths of rosebay willow herb, 'bombweed' as it was nicknamed."
>
> —*The New York Times*

Just like London after the Blitz,
when winter gave way
to sunlit spring,

so one day in Kharkiv,
wildflowers will bloom
among the rubble.

And yet, and yet,

years after *this* war has ended,
survivors will still tremble
at the flash and bang of bottle rockets
commemorating heroic victories.

ACKNOWLEDGMENTS

My gratitude to the courageous journalists whose on-the-ground reporting from embattled Ukraine informed many of these poems.

Some of these poems have appeared in the following publications:
Beltway Quarterly
Ibbetson #57
Juleboard #5
Mobius: A Journal of Social Change
The Arts Fuse
The Red Letters #234

MARK PAWLAK

who bears the surname of a grandfather born in Lviv, is the author of ten poetry collections, most recently *Away Away* (Arrowsmith Press, 2024), and the memoir *My Deniversity: Knowing Denise Levertov* (MadHat Press, 2021). His poems have been translated into German, Japanese, Polish, and Spanish, and have been performed at Teatr Polski in Warsaw. In English, his poems and prose have appeared widely in anthologies such as *The Best American Poetry*, *Blood to Remember: American Poets on the Holocaust*, *For the Time Being: The Bootstrap Anthology of Poetic Journals* and in the literary magazines *New American Writing*, *Mother Jones*, *Poetry South*, *The Saint Ann's Review*, and *The World*, among many others. He taught mathematics at the University of Massachusetts Boston (1979-2016), where he was Director of Academic Support Programs and received the Chancellors Achievement Award. He lives in Cambridge.

Mark Pawlak

SPECIAL OPERATION

Beltway EDITIONS

printing was completed in February 2026 for Beltway Editions